July 4. 2009 Aloha Victor...

MW01016984

Your friend,

HAWAIIAN BIRTHRIGHTS

UNDERSTANDING "HAWAIIAN NATIONAL", PRIVATE CITIZEN BIRTH RIGHTS

Aran Alton Ardaiz

Disclaimer

Author has noticed a
printing error of some
Hawaiian words in this
First Edition

Truth of God Ministry
Hawaiian Islands

Published by
Truth of God Ministry
Hawaiian Islands

General Delivery, (Box 62107)
Manoa Station, Island of Oahu
The Hawaiian Islands
(U.S.P.Z. Exempt)

ISBN 10: 0-615-29733-1
ISBN 13: 978-0-615-29733-0

HAWAIIAN BIRTHRIGHTS

UNDERSTANDING *"HAWAIIAN NATIONAL"*, PRIVATE CITIZEN BIRTH RIGHTS

A Nation under Ke Akua!

SUBJECT: THE JURISDICTIONAL DIFFERENCE AND USE BETWEEN THE ALL CAPITALIZED LEGAL FICTION AND PROPER ENGLISH LANGUAGE SPELLED BIRTH NAME.

Our Hawaiian born **"Private Citizen's"**[1] *"inalienable"*[2] birth rights are preserved under our Hawaiian National *"common-law"*[3] in

---

1 Private. Affecting or belonging to private individuals as distinct from public generally. Not official; not clothed with office. (Source: Black's Law Dict. 6th Ed. Page 1195)

2 Inalienable rights. Rights which are God ordained and which are not capable of being surrendered or transferred without the consent of the one possessing such rights; e.g. freedom of speech or religion, due process, and equal protection of the laws. (Source: Black's Law Dict. 6th Ed. Page 759)

3 Common law. The common law of the Hawaiian Kingdom Nation is best defined in this 1892 definition: Chapter LVII. An Act To

our lawfully spelled birth names... not in the ALL CAPITALIZED fiction name created, owned and used by the foreign, occupying U.S. Federal Government.

The basic, primary law of the Hawaiian Kingdom Nation is the "*common-law*". Also, the ***Word of Almighty God*** is the ultimate authority as affirmed in the Constitutions of 1840, 1852 and 1864. Example: "***That no law shall be enacted which is at variance with the word of the Lord Jehovah or at variance with the general spirit of His word. All laws of the Islands shall be in consistency with the general spirit of God's law.***" *(Article 1 of the Constitution of 1840)*.

It was out of respect and recognition of ***Ke Akua Mana Loa*** *(Almighty God)* that the Monarchs of the Hawaiian Kingdom properly and righteously placed the authority of the living, *Almighty God* above their own authority, the common-law and the legislated laws of the Kingdom.

The following is the lawful definition for Hawaiian National common-law:

By ***An Act of the Sessions (1892)***: To

Reorganize the Judiciary Department (of the de jure *Hawaiian Kingdom National Government*).

Section 5. *"The common law of England, as ascertained by English and American decisions, is hereby declared to be the common law of the Hawaiian Islands in all cases, except as otherwise expressly provided by the Hawaiian Constitution or laws, or fixed by Hawaiian judicial precedent, or established by Hawaiian national usage, provided however, that no person shall be subject to criminal proceedings except as provided by the Hawaiian laws."*

A PEOPLE OF GREAT LOVE AND PATIENCE

It is apparent that Kē Aku' ă has blessed the Hawaiian People with great alo'hă *(love, compassion)* for all people. Unfortunately, many foreigners have only seen the Hawaiian People's love and caring for their fellow man as an opportunity and justification to abuse a loving hand extended in Aloha and peace. The Hawaiian People have not just a deep, meaningful love relationship with Kē Aku' ă, but have a great patience as a people, while yet acknowledging a justified and righteous

3

indignation within, for those who continue to exploit them.

IT'S TIME FOR HAWAIIAN NATIONALS TO GRASP BIRTHRIGHT TRUTH!

First of all, *"Hawaiian Nationals"* are a people of many ethnicities born within a national jurisdiction of a sovereign state (Nation). Secondly, the *Islands of the Hawaiian Kingdom* have never, in any lawful manner, been transferred to the United States Government <u>as falsely claimed by the United States</u>. Exclusive jurisdictional Island ownership is still the rightful, lawful possession of *Hawaiian "Nationals"* and their de jure Government titled: ***Ko Hawaii Pae Aina (The Hawaiian Islands; Hawaiian Kingdom)***. **Therefore, Hawaii is a sovereign, yet foreign occupied, <u>National</u> state.**

Hawaiian ***"Natural Born Citizens"***[4] are *"Persons who are born within the jurisdiction of a national government, i.e., (Hawaiian Islands) in its territorial limits, or those born of citizens temporarily residing abroad."* These are by virtue of their birth, Hawaiian

---

4 **Natural born citizen.** (Source: Black's Law Dict. 6th Ed. Page 1026)

"Private Citizens"[5] *("Nationals")* under their living Hawaiian Kingdom National Government laws.

"Hawaiian Nationals"[6] are not *"Native Hawaiians"*. The title, *"Native Hawaiian"* is a foreign U.S. Federal Government created label *(or definition, implemented by the occupiers)* within the *Territorial Act for Hawaii (1900)* to classify Hawaiians of the koko *(blood)* as aboriginals. This act was designed, with bias, to isolate the Hawaiian National of the koko from all other ethnics who were nationals of the Kingdom. Reason: Only the Hawaiians of the koko have an undivided 1/3rd vested ownership interest in the land, not dispersed *(The Mahele)*.

In contrast to the above, *"Native Hawaiians" (e.g. aboriginals)* live on the land but they do not own their land. This concept was possibly a predetermined U.S. option to claim that a conquest had occurred instead of a U.S. invasion in violation of the Treaty

---

5 **Private (Citizen).** Affecting or belonging to private individuals, as distinct from the public generally. Not official; not clothed with office. (Source: Black's Law Dictionary, 6th Edition, Page 1195)

6 **Hawaiian National.** Pertaining to one born to the Islands of the Hawaiian Archipelago, whose birth rights are, by virtue of birth to the aina, is a Hawaiian National; or maintained by a nation as an organized whole or independent political unit: national affairs.

of 1850; <u>OR</u>, that by doing so, they could isolate the <u>Hawaiians of the koko</u> to cause them to sell out their 1/3rd vested interest somewhere down the road *(OHA, Nation within a Nation, etc.)* so as to manipulate a claim of the Hawaiian Islands as U.S. soil, just like they have done to the American Indians.

For Hawaiians to stand for their birth rights and inalienable rights is not rebellion, nor is it treason, it is called *"righteousness!"*[31]

<u>Righteousness is of Almighty God!</u>

Your Hawaiian birth right is God ordained, and as a *Hawaiian National, Private Citizen,* no one has authority to take those rights and liberties from you without your fullness of knowledge and explicit consent as to why! This right is based upon your having been born within the Islands of the Hawaiian Archipelago and the *de jure "common-law"* protection provided you by your birth Nation's laws.

THE UNITED STATES RECOGNIZES HAWAIIAN NATIONALS

Fact: *"Hawaiian Nationals"* **still own their land under their own de jure government laws and national citizenship rights.** Secondly, the de jure laws of the *Hawaiian National (Kingdom) Government* were never lawfully abrogated *(abolished, annulled or repealed)*, only pushed aside.

THE TERRITORIAL ACT (1930)

Therefore, because the land is still in Hawaiian ownership, not having ever lawfully transferred to the jurisdiction of the United States; *Hawaiian Nationals* still possess their rightful national citizenship birth rights as recognized and affirmed under the foreign U.S. Organic Act and Statehood Act.

The **U.S. Organic Act** *(Territorial Act of April 30, 1900, C339, 31 Stat 141)* *states:*

"Section 4. That all persons (created entities) *who were citizens* (lesser, U.S. "Emancipate Slave" status "citizens") *of the Republic of Hawaii on August twelfth, eighteen hundred and ninety-eight, are hereby declared to be*

7

citizens of the Territory of Hawaii." (Author's Note: Please notice that the statement only says they are *"declared to be citizens"*; it does not say that they *"are"* citizens. Secondly, the great majority of Hawaiians *(+/- 93% of the population)* were not citizens of the Republic of Hawaii; they were natural, birth right nationals of the Aina. **Their citizenship did not transfer.**)

Please also take notice that under this Section, dealing with citizenship, that *"Hawaiian Nationals"* **born to the Aina, who are** *"Private Citizens"*, **are ignored and not even mentioned.** Only *"persons"* who were already U.S. *"citizens"* were *"...declared to be citizens..."* of the U.S. and of the newly formed Territory by this Act (YOU MUST READ BLACK'S LAW DICTIONARY MEANINGS IN A LATER CHAPTER FOR THE MEANING OF A "PERSON"). **This Act never changed the citizenship of the Hawaiian Nationals who were still under the rightful, de jure laws of their Kingdom.**

THE STATEHOOD ACT (OF 1959)

Secondly, under the **Puppet Statehood Act** *(Admissions Act of March 18, 1959, Pub L 863,*

8

73 Stat 4) <u>citizenship of Hawaiian Nationals</u> <u>was likewise not changed</u>, and I quote:

"Section 19. Nothing contained in this Act shall operate to confer United States nationality, nor to terminate nationality (e.g. citizenship of Hawaiian born Nationals was not terminated) *heretofore lawfully acquired* (by natural birth to the Aina)*, or restore nationality heretofore lost under any law* (open door for Hawaiians to reinstate their inalienable birth rights taken away by devious, unlawful de facto State name change) *of the United States or under any treaty* (Treaty of 1850, et al) *to which the United States is or was a party."*

In essence, what is being said is that this law *(the Statehood Act)* does not change the lawful standing *and* rights of *"Hawaiian National Private Citizens"* <u>of natural birth to</u> <u>the Aina</u>.

"Hawaiian Nationals" are those born to the *Islands of the Hawaiian Archipelago* <u>who</u> <u>have not contracted away their birthrights, or</u> <u>have re-claimed their birthrights</u>. Those born to the aina are of all ethnicities. They consist of Hawaiian ethnics *(of koko),* Portuguese,

German, Italian, Japanese, Chinese, Korean, Basque, Swiss, Russian, Irish; et al, and includes all multi-racial mixtures of those ethnicities.

NOTICE: Present day Hawaiians *(of all ethnic backgrounds)* have without their knowledge and consent, and under extreme duress have had their birth names changed by a foreign, occupying government to convert them to a foreign U.S. second-class citizenship status while still living on their own national birth lands.

It therefore stands that those who have unlawfully been deprived of their rights *(by fraud)* have every right under *Section 19 of the Puppet Statehood Act* to recovery of those inalienable birthrights.

"Ua Mau Ke Ea O Ka Aina I Ka Pono"

DIFFERENT NAMES FOR DIFFERENT JURISDICTIONS OF LAW AND CITIZENSHIP

HOW TO CAPTURE HAWAIIAN BORN NATIONALS

There has been much misunderstood discussion and ignorance regarding the proper and / or lawful birth names versus the pseudonym *(fictitious)* ALL CAPITALIZED or partially CAPITALIZED names. Let's say that my name is *"Kawika Kane: Kahiapo"*[7]. **To be more specific, a powerful difference exists between my lawful, proper, English-language spelled birth name, *"Kawika Kane: Kahiapo"*, a *"Hawaiian National"* and *"Private Citizen"* born to the aina of the Kingdom; and the <u>foreign</u> U.S. Government created and <u>imposed</u> partial CAPITALIZED or all CAPITALIZED *"fictitious name"*[8]** *(The use of the colon [:] after the given names, historically and by proper language usage, denotes "of the" family or clan. Therefore the name would be*

---

7 Used as an example for the purpose establishing understanding.

8 Fictitious name. 1. created, taken, or assumed for the sake of concealment; not genuine; false: fictitious names. 2. of, pertaining to, or consisting of fiction; imaginatively produced or set forth; created by the imagination: a fictitious hero. (Source: Webster's Encyclopedic Unabridged Dictionary 2001 Edition)

11

interpreted and read as "Kawika Kane" of the "Kahiapo" family or clan.).

My Hawaiian birth name spelled in the proper English-language manner <u>reveals me to be a *"Private Citizen"*</u>. As a *Private Citizen (a Hawaiian born "national")* I am definitely not a U.S. immigrant, civil servant, public official, corporation, naturalized *"citizen"*, member of a foreign military or corporate officer on my own national birth soil. I, **Kawika Kane Kahiapo** *(Sample name)* am a *"Private Citizen"* who has not abandoned nor signed away my birth rights as a *"Hawaiian National"* (<u>except under extreme duress)</u> to become a foreign, created, Federal jurisdiction <u>fiction person</u> *(e.g. a U.S. public "citizen")* on my own national aina.

I repeat; my birth name when spelled in proper English-language upper and lower case letters, according to proper English language cursive and scripted usage, <u>reflects who I am</u>. The proper spelling of my birth name affirms me to be a *"Private Citizen"* under my *Hawaiian National Government "common-law"* with my birth rights intact. **As a Hawaiian born *"National"* <u>with birth</u>**

rights I am under my lawful 1864 Constitution. I am not a foreign *"citizen"* under the *"Civil Rights Acts"* of the foreign U.S. military jurisdiction, without birth rights, just because some foreigner says I am.

I KNOW WHO I AM;
DO YOU KNOW WHO YOU ARE?

By natural birth, I am not the legally created, fictitious *"corporate person,"* titled and improperly printed as "**KAWIKA KANE KAHIAPO**"; or "**Kawika Kane KAHIAPO**" on foreign identification cards used by both foreign *(puppet state and federal)* occupying governments on my native soil. The printed ALL CAPITALIZED spelling of my name reflects an improper, grammatically abusive spelling of my proper birth name. It was a created fiction name for America's *Emancipated Slaves* under the *(1868)* 14th Amendment of the American Constitution by the U.S. Congress to provide those *Emancipated Slaves* a distinctively different, yet much lesser, U.S. *"Federal"* citizenship without State's birth rights.

The foreign U.S. Government owns that fictitious creation which it implements on my Hawaiian National Aina. It reflects a foreign U.S. citizenship <u>without U.S. birth rights</u>, and if I accept it, <u>it takes away my *Hawaiian National* birth rights</u>.

I find the <u>created fiction name</u> is primarily utilized on Hawaiian Aina to convert and subject us Hawaiian *"Nationals"* to U.S. Government authority by erasing my **"inalienable"**[9] birth rights and changing the jurisdiction of law and flag that I thought I was submitted to *(Hawaiian National Flag)*, to one that is foreign to my birth rights *(the 50 star flag of the U.S. Military)*.

TWO TYPES OF CITIZENSHIP

There are two (2) types of citizenship in the Hawaiian Islands and have been since before the U.S. supported unlawful, 1893 overthrow of the Kingdom Government. **There is the *"Hawaiian National"* born to the Islands <u>with birth rights</u>**; and, there is the foreign created and imposed, U.S. Federal fiction *"<u>citizen</u>"*, type of citizenship, <u>without birth rights</u>.

---

9 **Inalienable.** Inalienable rights are those rights which are not capable of being surrendered or transferred without my consent being the one possessing such rights; e.g., freedom of speech or religion, due process, and equal protection of the laws; (the common-law) right to a jury of my peers, right to travel ect. (Source: Black's Law Dict. 6th Ed. Page 759)

MY LAND IS STILL MY LAND

I was born on the Island of Oahu in *"Ko Hawaii Pae Aina" (The Hawaiian Islands)*, a sovereign, foreign occupied, *"**Nation State**"*[10]. My birth rights are not determined by a foreign government unlawfully occupying my nation, but by the *de jure* laws of my *Hawaiian National Government* which rightfully still possesses **"*exclusive territorial jurisdiction*"**[11] *(e.g. the, rightful ownership of my national birth land)*.

The U.S. Federal Government and military also does not even lawfully possess *"**extraterritorial jurisdiction**"*[12] *(lawful right to extend its authority and power)* over the Hawaiian Islands without lawful *(de jure)* *Hawaiian National Government* consent, which it does not possess.

---

10 Sovereign state. States whose subjects or citizens are in the habit of obedience to them, and which are not themselves subject to any other (or paramount) state in any respect. The state is said to be semi-sovereign only, and not sovereign, when in any respect or respects it is liable to be controlled by a paramount government... (Black's Law Dict. 6th Ed. Page 1396)

11 Exclusive territorial jurisdiction. The highest form of jurisdictional land control, not limited. Possessing the sole, exclusive possession of a land or territory within a particular country. – Author.

12 Extraterritorial. Beyond the physical and juridical boundaries of a particular state or country (Example: U.S.). See Extraterritoriality. (Source: Black's Law Dictionary, 6th Ed. Page 588)

15

Therefore, the de facto Puppet STATE OF HAWAII does not own my Island Nation's land because the U.S. Government has never lawfully had *"leasehold"*, *"limited"* or *"original"* jurisdiction over my Hawaiian National lands, even though falsely claimed.

I could only have been born on Hawaiian National Aina.

I am, by virtue of my birth in the *Hawaiian Islands*, protected by my *Hawaiian Kingdom "common-law"*, my *Hawaiian Government* and my *Hawaiian National Constitution*, as a *"Hawaiian National and Private Citizen"*.

I am not a foreign second-class, immigration status, federal U.S. *"public citizen"* under, Article 1 Section 8 of a <u>foreign</u> nation's Constitution; just because some corrupt foreign official, unlawfully person or entity on my birth land says I am; <u>and has unlawfully changed my birth name and Birth Certificate to a fiction name for that unlawful purpose</u>.

HAWAII NOT A LAWFUL STATE

The *de facto* Puppet STATE OF HAWAII

is a pretentious entity without land; deceptively and unlawfully created by the U.S. Federal Government for U.S. Federal military use and for fiction *"citizens"* living on and unlawfully occupying my Hawaiian National Aina. The fake Puppet State of Hawaii was not created for Hawaiian *"Nationals"* like me.

EVERY CITIZEN HAS THE RIGHT TO BE FREE IN HIS OWN COUNTRY

CITIZENSHIP IS VOLUNTARY, NOT MANDATORY!

Don't forget this fact.

"...That this nation, under God, shall have
a new birth of freedom..."

- *Abraham Lincoln*

THE (HAWAIIAN)
U.S. FEDERAL "citizen"
HAS NO BIRTH RIGHTS

A *"public citizen"* or U.S. *"person"* is a U.S. Federal *"citizen"* under the *U.S. Civil Rights Acts (legislated and statutory law)* and Article 1 Sec. 8 of the Constitution of the American Republic. IF I were a U.S. "citizen"; I would be a fiction ***"person"***[13] as well, without full constitutional rights or protection under the *American Constitution of the Republic.* Under the fiction name I would be a second-class immigrant, a naturalized *"citizen"*, a civil servant, public official, officer of a corporation, or member of the military, et cetera even on U.S. soil.

MY GOVERNMENT
IS ALIVE IN ME

But I am not on U.S. soil! Therefore, as a *"Private Citizen"* born to *Hawaiian* soil, I am automatically a *"Hawaiian National*

---

13 **Person.** In general usage, a human being (i.e. natural person), though by statute term may include labor organizations, partnerships, associations, corporations, legal representatives, trustees, trustees in bankruptcy, or receivers... (Source: Black's Law Dict. 6th Ed., Page 1142.) Author's Clarifying Note: Under the common-law, you are a "natural 'person" or living human being. Under the civil law, you are a U.S. Federal "corporate person", "citizen", and corporation etc., not a living human being, a fiction.

Private Citizen" and am under the *"common-law"* of the 1864 *Constitution* of my de jure *Hawaiian National (Kingdom) Government.* My birth right is that of being born to one of the *Islands of the Hawaiian Archipelago*; and is not that being forcefully imposed, under extreme duress, by an occupying foreign nation unlawfully using created fake names and falsified birth certificates to convert and capture my *Hawaiian National, Private Citizen* birth rights.

HAWAIIAN IDENTIFICATION

We Hawaiian National Private Citizens must strive to obtain and use *Hawaiian National Government* issued identification cards revealing our lawful birth names, properly spelled, under our own living Hawaiian National laws and our own Hawaiian National Flag.

If I had been born in Washington D.C., or any of the military jurisdictions or federal states *(e.g. territories like American Samoa, Guam, Puerto Rico [Panama], or American Virgin Islands)*, or a corporate entity, using the CAPITALIZED NAME, I would be a U.S. Federal *"public citizen"*, or *"person"* under

Article 1 Section 8 jurisdiction *(e.g. public servant, civil service, military and corporate officers)* of the American Constitution, AND, while in that jurisdiction, I would be a foreigner to my *Hawaiian National Constitution* and also to the *American Constitution of the Republic* due to the simple lack of a birth right. **This differentiation is affirmed by the simple convoluted spelling of my name.**

YOUR MILITARY NAME

If I served in the foreign United States Military *(To protect the American People who lived under the Constitutions of the several States, e.g. Union of States)*, my name would be deliberately changed into the printed ALL CAPITALIZED LETTERS to formally identify me as being outside of the American Constitution *(as a federally contracted, subordinate rights citizen)*. I would also be temporarily forfeiting my constitutional *Hawaiian National* birth rights by simply submitting by contract to the foreign federal military flag jurisdiction and rule. By making this more personal, I hope to help you better understand just what has happened to our Hawaiian National

21

"Private Citizen" birth rights, freedoms and liberties.

My properly spelled birth name, when scripted *(written out in cursive)* is my lawful *"seal"*.[14] It grants or denies authority to others; it obligates or denies rights in contract format. It is my seal as a *Hawaiian National* affirming my authority as a *Private Citizen* under the living *(1864) Constitution of the Hawaiian Kingdom* based upon my natural birth on one of the *Islands of the Hawaiian Archipelago, my Nation.*

MY INALIENABLE RIGHTS

My Hawaiian National Constitutional Rights and *"inalienable"*[15] birth rights are protected and preserved in my properly spelled birth name! As a Hawaiian National, I have inalienable rights under my lawful 1864 National Constitution. My inalienable rights are my rights which are not capable of being surrendered or transferred without my explicit consent being the one possess-

---

14 **Seal.** An impression upon wax, wafer, or some other tenacious substance capable of being impressed. In current practice, a particular sign (e.g. L.S. [Lawful Signature].) or the word "seal" is made in lieu of an actual seal to attest the execution of the instrument. .. (Black's Law Dict. 6th Ed. Page 1348)

15 **Inalienable rights.** (Source: Black's Law Dict. 6th Ed. Page 759)

ing such rights; e.g., freedom of speech or religion, due process, and equal protection of the laws; the common-law right to a jury of my peers, right to travel et cetera. No one can take those rights from me, <u>but I can still reject them, abandon them, or forfeit them with or without my explicit consent</u>. It is called contracting away my birth rights.

Under *Hawaiian Kingdom National law*, absolutely no other citizen, person or entity *(foreign government or its local puppet)* has power to change my birth name to a fiction. <u>That right is mine and mine alone</u>. Even a great foreign power like the U.S. does not have that unlawful right over me, a *Hawaiian born National*. Yet, under present excessive *abuse of power* and *abuse of police power* while under United States occupation <u>causing extreme duress</u>, as mentioned, it has been different.

If I was an *American National,* I could under *Article 1 Section 10* of the *American Constitution of the Republic (foreign law)* contract my rights away. **I am a Hawaiian National! This U.S. Constitutional Article <u>was not written for *Hawaiian Nationals*</u> who are foreign to both American National and**

U.S. Federal jurisdictions. Unfortunately, this Article of the American Constitution is deviously used by the <u>lesser</u> U.S. Federal Government to take *Hawaiian National Private Citizens* as well as *American National Private Citizens* out from under their natural birth names, birth rights and <u>National Flags</u>. It's done in order to capture them through their ignorance and move their citizenship into the <u>lesser</u> foreign U.S. federal *(military)* jurisdiction within Article 1 Section 8 *(a jurisdiction of law foreign to their birth)* under the foreign <u>50 star federal military flag</u> *(e.g. as "public citizens"/"Taxpayers" of Washington D.C.)*.

TWO FLAGS – ONE IS FOREIGN!

MY FLAG OF THE
HAWAIIAN NATION
MY NATIONAL FLAG

The National Flag of the Hawaiian King-
dom is seen on the Cover of this Booklet.
Its dimension is 1:2 or one dimension high
by two in length. It is the lawful flag of my
Hawaiian Nation. **The Hawaiian Flag on the
Cover of this Booklet is my flag!**

THEIR IMPOSTER FLAG

There is another flag that looks like the
Hawaiian Kingdom National Flag, but it
is not. It is an imitation closely designed
to look the same. That flag is the de facto
(unlawful, but in power) Puppet STATE OF
HAWAII flag. It is different in length. It is
approximately 1:1.9 or, one dimension high
by one and nine-tenths long. It looks like
the *Hawaiian National Flag*, but it is not. It
is a foreign flag that is made to look like
the Hawaiian National Flag for a reason....
most people do not know the difference, but
the "**law of the flag**"[16] applies. I will quote

16 **Law of the Flag.** (Source: Black's Law Dictionary, 6th Edition, Page 638.)

25

the definition on flag law: *"In maritime law, the law of that nation or country whose flag is flown by a particular vessel. A ship owner who sends his vessel into a foreign port gives notice by his flag to all who enter into contracts with his master that he intends the law of that flag to regulate such contracts, and that they must either submit to its operation or not contract with him."* (***This would apply to not just a boat or ship, but also to the sanctuary of a courtroom or any enclosed sanctuary, assembly or room where the flag is flown. – Author***)

CITIZENSHIP IS VOLUNTARY

UNDERSTANDING "HAWAIIAN NATIONAL", PRIVATE
CITIZENSHIP BIRTH RIGHTS

ABOUT THAT FOREIGN, MILITARY CREATED, 50 STAR FLAG

Hawaii and Alaska <u>were supposed to become</u> States of the American Union, a Republic. Unfortunately, the *50 Star U.S. Federal Government military flag* was <u>unlawfully created</u> by supposedly adding two (2) stars to the *48 Star Flag of the American Republic and its Union of States* to create a *"military flag"[17]* along with the yellow fringe. The truth is; <u>a completely new</u> U.S. Federal jurisdiction military flag was created <u>unlawfully</u> by the unilateral action of then Commander-in-Chief, Dwight Eisenhower and not by the *National Congress of the Republic* as required by the American Constitution and *"Positive law"*. The Commander-in-Chief of the United States Military under **Executive Order No. 10834** on **8-25-59**, created the new *federal fifty star military jurisdiction flag*. It is a flag foreign to even American national State's rights jurisdiction.

Under Title 4, Section 1 of the United States

---

[17] **Military flag.** 1925 United States Attorney General Opinion No. 34, regarding military flag use. (4 USC 1, (1925 footnote) 34 Op Atty Gen 483. Also affirmed in 4 USCA (Annotated) Sections 1 and 2.

Code (Positive law) the lawful American Flag of the Republic and Union of States is still 48 Stars. If Hawaii really was a State of the Union, why wasn't the Positive law changed to reveal that change? <u>Reason</u>: It was created by the President acting as the military Commander-In-Chief and not by the National Congress of the Union of States.

The 50 star flag, because of its unlawful creation, is in fact, a *military flag*, with or without a yellow fringe on its perimeter.

When yellow fringe is placed around the perimeter of the Forty-Eight (48) Star Flag of the American Republic, it also becomes a military flag. The *<u>yellow fringe</u>* mutilates *<u>(makes unlawful)</u>* the American Flag as affirmed by **Title 4 USC Section 3** by either attachment of fringe, adding a third color, or both.

Under the <u>Positive law</u> of Title 4, Section 1, of the United States Code, the President of the U.S. has a lawful limit. <u>He can only arrange the stars</u> on the *Positive law, American Flag of the Republic.* **<u>An American President has no lawful right or authority to add stars OR create a new flag for Americans.</u>**

28

That right is reserved solely to the *National Congress* of the Union of States *(We the People)* under the U.S. Constitution for the Republic.

TRUTH IS MORE POWERFUL THAN THE LIE

"Today, many Peoples of Hawaii, forgetting or not knowing their rich past; not knowing their rightful citizenship; fearfully oppressed by foreign imposed income taxes and excessive land taxes by de facto, lesser (foreign controlled) local governments; blinded by creature comforts; dependent upon foreign commerce and false promises by a foreign nation holding them hostage; have been sold into slavery for their land – <u>without their awareness</u>."

-Author

"Where the people fear the government
you have tyranny; where the government
fears the people, you have liberty."

- *Thomas Jefferson*

BACK TO THAT NAME THING CREATED FOR "EMANCIPATED SLAVES"

The improper English language pseudonym or alias name was created in order to distinguish the ***"Emancipated Slave"*** *(a created federal "public citizen")* from the Caucasian *"American National Private Citizen" ("sovereign").* The *"Emancipated Slave"* was a supposedly freed slave as designated by Abraham Lincoln's *Emancipation Proclamation* issued on January 1, 1863, declaring that all persons held in slavery in certain designated states and districts were and should remain free. White biased Americans then in power considered Hawaiians as dark skinned, or, "blacks". That fact is easily deduced historically by the treatment and character of U.S. abuse of Hawaiians as a People.

That devious application of name change worked so well in America for controlling *"Emancipated Slaves"* that the U.S. Government decided to apply that manipulation of birth rights on *Private Citizens* of the Hawaiian Kingdom. It worked! It was implemented without either challenge or understanding resulting in Hawaiian Nationals *(Private Citizens)* in ignorance, fraudulently being induced to sign away their <u>Hawaiian National birthright citizenship</u>, and inalienable rights while also being deprived of justice in the U.S. controlled courts.

<u>THE "NEW 1869 SLAVE ACT"</u> DO SLAVES HAVE BIRTHRIGHTS?

No! <u>Slaves did not then nor do they now possess any type of birth right citizenship</u> ... they are possessions, e.g. *"things",* hence the 1869, 14th Amendment Congress <u>creation of the artificial</u> federal *"public citizen".* Do you have birth rights? Are you a slave? By what printed name do you identify yourself? Remember, the U.S. Federal created fiction type *"citizen"* does not possess Constitutional rights *(neither State nor Federal),* State's birth rights or even inalienable rights and freedoms... even on American soil! It is definitely inferior to the sovereign State's rights birth citizenship possessed by ***"natural"*** [18] born Caucasian

---

18 **Natural born.** Natural born citizen. Persons who are born within the jurisdiction of a national government, i.e., in its territorial limits, or those born of citizens temporarily residing abroad. (Source: Black's Law Dictionary 6th Ed., Page 1026)

Congressmen of that period.

Because the fiction *"citizen"*, *"person"* or *"thing"* was created by the United States Government; it *(e.g. the name and the person it is attached to)* are in fact, owned or possessed *(enslaved?)* by the United States Federal Government! It is the government's name and *"person"* to legally own by creation, **"custom and usage"**[19].

Since World War II and before, the truth and distinction between types of citizenship has been cautiously and deliberately removed from our textbooks in our grammar schools, high schools and colleges. Therefore, how can you be expected to make intelligent decisions when the facts requiring that knowledge of citizenship and rights have been deliberately hidden from you? You cannot! You're ignorant not because you do not have the mental capability to

---

19 Custom and (common) usage. Definition - U.C.C. § 1-205[2]: "A usage or practice of the people, which, by common adoption and acquiescence, and by long and unvarying habit, has become compulsory, and has acquired the force of law with respect to the place and subject-matter to which it relates. It results from a long series of actions, constantly repeated, which have, by such repetition and by uninterrupted acquiescence, acquired the force of a tacit and common consent. A parole evidence rule does not bar evidence of custom or usage to explain or supplement a contract or memorandum of the parties."

comprehend and make intelligent decisions, but because you have been denied the very truth and knowledge necessary upon which to make those intelligent and competent decisions. This deliberate, programmed action is open corruption by those supposed political public servants elected, appointed and hired to serve us.

The lawful, proper spelling in the English language of the birth name given me by my parents at birth is my lawful identity.

As a child, under Hawaiian law, until the age of consent or age permitted for lawful contract, no person or government has the authority to modify or change my name, except me. Again, this is my identity...this is who I am! It is very, very personal. It tells all others in the world that I am lawfully distinct from all of them. If changed without my consent due to my ignorance that that change creates, that becomes an unlawful act of fraud against me. If done in an organized, programmed and deliberate manner to achieve an unlawful affect or advantage over me, a living soul *(a "living soul" or "human being" as differentiated from the created "thing", or "fictitious person"),* that becomes what is known under law as, *"**constructive fraud**"*,[20] a criminal offense. It is identity theft on a massive scale exercised through government fraud and corruption. It is theft of my birthright, birth name, Hawaiian National rights and God given inalienable rights *(freedoms)*! <u>All this corruption is endorsed and executed with the fullness of knowledge by Hawaii's elected politicians, their corrupt, liberal minded, Godless judges, legal professionals, et al; who lie, refusing truthfulness and honesty, and most definitely lacking integrity</u>!

What I believe is so wonderfully unique about the proper, lawful birth name is that it provides me with lawfully protected <u>inalienable</u>, God given rights and liberties!

Birth rights are first of all determined by the following:

    a) Natural heritage *(Citizenship)* of my parents.

---

20 Constructive fraud. Exists where conduct, though not actually fraudulent, has all actual consequences and all legal effects of actual fraud…. Breach of legal or equitable duty which, irrespective of moral guilt, is declared by law to be fraudulent because of its tendency to deceive others or violate confidence. (Source: Black's Law Dict. 6th Ed., Page 314)

b) The land of my birth *(Nation)*
c) The proper spelling of my birth name which guarantees me my inalienable birth rights.

CITIZENSHIP IS VOLUNTARY

CONTRACTING AWAY
YOUR CHILD'S AND YOUR
OWN BIRTH RIGHTS

A living soul *(a human being)*, under the laws of *"Ke Aupuni O Hawaii Nei"*[21], cannot lawfully change his or her birth name until the age permitted by law for lawful right to contract. That age is twenty-one (21) years. Therefore, any change to the lawful birth name by convoluted spelling *(or changes of any kind)* is not lawful if done prior to that lawful age of the right to contract. This is an important point – DON'T FORGET THIS FACT OF LAWFUL RIGHT.

In today's society, children *(not "kids": kids = goats)* are not taught the basics of grammar, the importance of their birth names or the importance of their citizenship rights under Almighty God.

In what is most often a misunderstood usage by *Peoples of the Hawaiian Islands* is the name *"American"*. Most Hawaiians *(and Americans)* born to the aina today walk with the presumption that they are in

---

21 **Ke Aupuni O Hawaii Nei.** Translated: The Government of all Hawaii. (Hawaiian Kingdom)

fact, *"American National Private Citizens"*
when in fact they are not! If you as a parent
have given away your children's birth name
and assumed for them the fiction ALL
CAPITALIZED NAME identity, you have
in fact given away their *Hawaiian National*
or *American National Private Citizenship*
status *(as well as their inalienable rights)* e.g.
birth rights.

WHAT ABOUT MY BIRTH RIGHTS?

What about my birthrights? What did I just
say? I said, I can call myself a *"Hawaiian"*
or an *"American"* but, have I permitted my
name to be converted or changed *(Either
with or without my explicit, written consent)*
to the printed ALL CAPITALIZED
(fictitious name)? If so, I would not be
the *"Hawaiian National Private Citizen"*
or *"American National Private Citizen"* I
thought myself to be. I will have converted
myself into a lesser, second-class U.S.
immigration status *"fiction citizen"* foreign
to my national birth rights and Hawaiian
National protective *"**common law**."*[22]

The Hawaiian *"common law"* provides me

---

[22] Hawaiian common law. See Page 3

my inalienable *"Private Citizen"* status under the Hawaiian National Constitution! The national *"common-law" (as distinguished from statutory law which is created by the enactment of legislatures)* comprises the body of those principles and rules of action, relating to the government and security of persons and property, which derive their authority solely from usages and customs of immemorial antiquity, or from the judgments and decrees of the courts recognizing, affirming and enforcing such usages and customs; and, in this sense, particularly the ancient unwritten law of England. <u>In general, it is a body of law that develops and derives through judicial decisions</u>, as distinguished from legislative enactments. The *"common law"* is all the statutory and case law background of England and the American colonies *(since)* before the American Revolution. It consists of those principles, usage and rules of actions applicable to government and security of persons and property which do not rest for their authority upon any express and positive declaration of the will of the legislature. ***The Hawaiian Kingdom common law is printed on Page 3.***

WHAT'S YOUR IDENTITY?

As stated, <u>if</u> you identify yourself as a 14th Amendment, U.S. Federal *"thing"* or *"public citizen"* outside of your countries birth jurisdiction, you no longer possess your *"inalienable rights"*; <u>you would only possess federal</u> U.S. <u>legislated</u> and <u>statutory</u> *"Civil Rights"*, just like the freed *"Emancipated slaves"* after and since the Civil War. You will have lowered and abandoned your greater Hawaiian National birth right standard of citizenship!

So, have you given away your Hawaiian *"natural"* birth rights? Are you now under Article 1, Sections 8 and 10 of the foreign U.S. Constitution of that foreign, military jurisdiction of law that unlawfully occupies the Hawaiian Islands? The U.S. federal jurisdiction *(military)* is supposed to protect the *American National Private Citizen* e.g. sovereign *(one under his lawful, English language spelled birth name)*, from America's foreign enemies. **This U.S. manipulation of rights is not designed to and most definitely does not protect *Hawaiian Nationals* on Hawaiian Aina.**

When discharged from the military, we are released from the <u>contracted</u> active duty military service and from under the <u>contracted</u>, printed, ALL CAPITALIZED fiction name to return to our birth names where our birth rights *(inalienable rights)* are protected *(under various State of the Union "common-laws" or)* Hawaii's National *"common law"*. Since you left the U.S. military did you recapture your properly spelled birth name wherein your inalienable rights as a *Hawaiian National* and *Private Citizen* are preserved? Think!

BIBLICAL BIRTHRIGHT TRANSFER

In the Holy Scriptures, Genesis 25: 30-34, *"Esau despised his birth right"* because he didn't see any immediate *"profit"*. The benefit to him was far away and he saw it as a responsibility not worth the contract *(Covenant)* God had ordained. Under the Law of God, all of his father's *(Isaac's)* assets would be his, as would the responsibilities of his mother and the minor children, if any. Responsibility is something Esau didn't want or he would have valued his birth right, which was his, being the first born, by law and custom. He didn't care.

Why have we neglected our birth right citizenship? Like Esau, do we really not want responsibility for our birth rights and freedoms? How did we get where we are? Do we want to stay there? Really, it all depends on how we see and value our birth rights, freedoms and citizenship.

WHERE IS YOUR SECURITY?

Question: Is your security in the many, many false and inflated foreign government promises and an uncertain promised future financial security or in your Hawaiian National birthrights given to you by Almighty God?

Devious, misguided politically influenced, ignorant people in the de facto *"corporate"* state judiciary and *"corporate"* federal government *(civil service servants)* operating within the statutory jurisdiction of the Federal United States *(the Article 1 Sections 8 and 10, 50 star military flag jurisdiction)* deliberately modify and change the names of *Hawaiian Nationals* at birth for a reason. They can create tax paying *"non-persons"* *(e.g. "citizens" "corporations", and other "things" which are fictions)*.

THEY CREATE FICTION CITIZENS

Governments cannot create human life. They can only create fictions like legal persons without birth rights, corporations, corporate persons etc. I qualify a *"non-person"* as any one of these.

The foreign Puppet Hawaii State and federal U.S. Government civil servants, following orders from above, readily convert *Hawaiian National Private Citizens,* who have been kept ignorant, into lesser, *"U.S. second-class, immigration status "federal, corporate, legal fiction 'citizens'"* in order to remove them from their inalienable rights inherent by Hawaiian National natural birth so as to burden them with foreign taxes and control them. This devious conversion is accomplished <u>by utilizing the fiction name that sounds the same, but is not</u>. This newly applied *"legal fiction"* name is then identified with the Hawaiian *"living soul"* or natural man who fails to distinguish the difference. Your signature *(seal)* on a document having on it the printed fiction, partial or ALL CAPITALIZED, name gives/grants your acknowledgement and approval by formal endorsement of the fiction name, as your own.

SCRIPTING THE ALL CAP NAME

Such an improper spelling of one's name is not a proper use of the English language, which is a scripted language, as mentioned previously. The proof of that fact is that it cannot be written *(scripted, written in cursive)*. You cannot script or write a name created in the printed ALL CAPITALIZED format only because the capitalized letters begin with a short down stroke or a short upstroke and when tied together will go up and down on a page and not in a straight line, which is not proper English cursive writing. <u>It therefore serves as a substitute alias, a deliberately created fiction, unlawfully utilized</u>. It is also called a *"nom de guerre"*, or, *"name of war"*, having come to use off of tombstones… that of a dead man.

This improper, unlawful renaming of the *Hawaiian National Private Citizen, "a living soul"* or natural man without his or her fullness of awareness, knowledge and <u>explicit</u> consent as to the consequences, is fraud! The de facto, Puppet STATE OF HAWAII and the foreign U.S. Federal Government functioning jointly on sovereign *Hawaiian National Government* soil cannot lawfully convert you, *"a living soul"* into a *"fiction"* or *"thing"* to manipulate you as their own without your fullness of knowledge and agreement, **e.g. "*consent*"** [23] *(a concurrence of the wills).* They do it to you out of your ignorance and your misguided trust in their corrupt system.

The reason they do horrible, demonic acts of deception and oppression is because the foreign Federal United States Government and Court systems *(lesser jurisdiction Article 1 Courts)* do not have lawful authority over the *Hawaiian National; a Private Citizen (living soul and natural man).* The wise Hawaiian functions with lawful knowledge under his properly spelled birth right name, identification, Hawaiian National Flag and Kingdom laws.

NOTICE: If you subject your proper, natural birth name citizenship to a foreign flag jurisdiction of law, you loose your rights

---

23 Consensual contract. A term derived from the civil law, denoting a contract founded upon and completed by the mere consent of the contracting parties, without any external formality or symbolic act to fix the obligation. (Source: Black's Law Dict. 6th Ed. Page 304.)

by acquiescence and become subject to the laws of that foreign country or jurisdiction *(or court)*. This is your choice and your right! Remember, only the U.S. Federal Government functions under the *"legal fiction"* name and their fiction flag because they have authority over the *"thing"* and corporations, ect, that they create and own.

CITIZENSHIP IS VOLUNTARY

THE U.S. GOVERNMENT CREATED FICTION "PERSON" UNDER THE FIFTY STAR MILITARY FLAG

FOR HAWAIIAN CITIZEN AWARENESS

The U.S. Government created fiction *"person"*[24] is a federal *"citizen"* of Washington D.C., its territories, military and corporate entities. Let me define *"Person"* from the original First and Second Editions of Black's Law Dictionaries. The later editions, including the 6th Edition of Black's Law Dictionary cloud the real meaning of *"person"*.

(Black's First Edition) *Person. "A man considered according to the rank he holds in society, with all the rights to which the place he holds entitles him, and the duties which it imposes. 1 Bouv. Inst. No. 137. A human being considered as capable of having rights and being charged with duties; while a "thing" is*

---

24 Person. In general usage, a human being (i.e. natural person), though by statute term may include labor organizations, partnerships, associations, corporations, legal representatives, trustees, trustees in bankruptcy, or receivers... (Source: Black's Law Dict. 6th Ed., Page 1142.) Author's Clarifying Note: Under the common-law, you are a "natural 'person" or living human being. Under the civil law, you are a U.S. Federal "corporate person", "citizen", and corporation etc., not a living human being, a fiction.

the object over which rights may be exercised. Persons are divided by law into natural and artificial. Natural persons are such as the God of nature formed us; artificial are such as are created and devised by human laws, for the purposes of society and government, which are called "corporations" or "bodies politic." 1 Bl. Comm. 123."

(Black's Second Edition) Same as above definition but more so clarifies "*Person*" as:

*—Artificial persons. Such as are created and devised by law for the purposes of society and government, called "corporations" or "bodies politic." - **Natural persons.** Such as are formed by nature, as distinguished from artificial persons, or corporations. — **Private person.** An individual who is not the incumbent of an office."*

Therefore, <u>the created fiction *"person"*</u> is distinctly different in rights at law from that of the living soul *(living natural person, e.g. "human being")* e.g. Hawaiian *National Private Citizen.* The *Hawaiian National,* on his own soil, has superior rights in both law and citizenship to that of the U.S. Federal *"corporate legal fiction created" "person"* with the printed, partial or ALL CAPITALIZED fictitious, alias name. Remember, the *"legal fiction name"* is that of a second-class, immigration status United States *"federal fiction person, citizen or thing"* and is used to legally separate you from your Hawaiian and/or American Constitution and inalienable birth rights.

FICTIONS ARE NOT UNDER THE 48 STAR FLAG OF THE REPUBLIC

At this time, The U.S. Federal *"legal fiction citizen"* is not under the *Positive law, 48 Star Flag of the American Republic*. He is, as a *"citizen"* of Washington D.C. under the lesser constitutional federal jurisdiction. He most definitely is a lesser status, fiction *"person"* and not an American National.

The unlawfully created new 50 star flag is a lesser in right flag representing only the constitutionally limited federal military jurisdiction, as opposed to the greater *Positive law*, 48 Star Union Flag of the Republic representing all of America's independent, sovereign States AND federal jurisdictions.

49

FACT: The American Flag of Forty-Eight Stars is still alive and is the *Positive law* Flag of the American Union of States, a Republic.

HAWAII IS A U.S. MILITARY OCCUPIED JURISDICTION

With or without the yellow fringe, the *fifty star flag* is still only a <u>lesser</u>, federal jurisdiction military flag. Please note that this *fifty star military flag* with military fringe *(denoting military occupation)* flies in the courtrooms of the de facto Puppet STATE OF HAWAII and in all Article 1 *(lesser)* federalized de facto state courts and offices.

As in the present *de facto, Puppet* HAWAII STATE, the present ***U.S. Court for the Hawaii District*** also functions under the yellow fringed 50 star military flag of occupation. <u>It is a deceptive, pretentious court, at most.</u>[30] The *"**U.S. Court for the Hawaii District"* is not under the Constitution of the American Republic"* as falsely stipulated <u>in writing</u> within the Puppet Hawaii State Constitution *(it is not the proper Article III Court as specifically misrepresented therein).* The *U.S. Court for the Hawaii District's* lawfully <u>defined jurisdiction does not</u>

incorporate any of the Hawaiian Islands of the Archipelago within its authority, nor are its judges under lawful oaths of office as required by American law.

Therefore, I believe, the _abuse of police power_ _(the type of control)_ exercised over the Hawaiian People of the Islands is still the same as that exercised by the de facto _Republic of Hawaii,_ the overthrow entity!

CITIZENSHIP IS VOLUNTARY

"If you do not know your birthrights and your citizenship rights, you are not free; you are either being led,or dead!"

- _Author_

THE RIGHT TO VOTE AND THE RIGHT TO FREE SPEECH ARE INALIENABLE RIGHTS

DOES A POLICE STATE EXIST IN HAWAII?

Answer: For Hawaiians of the koko, "Yes!" Most Hawaiians *(of all ethnicities)* born to the islands today have by deception become Federal United States *"corporate created fiction citizens"* without their knowledge and awareness. Many are probably content to be so, many are not... but again, don't forget, **CITIZENSHIP IS VOLUNTARY. If not, we are all bound prisoners within a foreign *"police state"*[25] U.S. Federal (Military) Government, without rights.** Hawaiians of the koko, et al, are deliberately suppressed and fall into this latter category.

A police state condition exists when police power entrusted to civil government *(the de facto Puppet State of Hawaii)* is exercised to excess, and abusive in violation of the inalienable *Hawaiian* and/or *American National* Constitutional rights of the Hawaiian or American born *"National", "Private Citizen" (whose rights are today, greatly infringed upon and denied)*.

---

25 Police state. A nation in which the police, esp. a secret police, summarily suppresses any social, economic or political act that conflicts with governmental policy. (Source: Webster's Encyclopedic Unabridged Dictionary, 2001 Ed.)

The taking away of a Private Citizen's national birth rights *(e.g. inalienable rights)* is a deliberately deceptive practice presently implemented by the de facto puppet state and U.S. Federal Governments on Hawaiian Aina. The denial of the Hawaiian and American National's inalienable rights to justice, to travel, to vote, to worship Almighty God, to common law trial by a jury of Peers, unlawful arrest and imprisonment, etc. are just some examples of the presently used <u>abuse of police power</u> exercised collectively by Hawaiian State and local police, politicians, attorneys and judiciaries, with U.S. Government approval.

<u>You have the lawful right to peacefully separate yourself *(cancel the contract)* from the alien federal military jurisdiction</u>, just as you can be and/or get discharged from the U.S. Military <u>contract</u> and return to your home island of birth, your inalienable rights and your lawful birth name, leaving the unauthorized legal, temporary corruption of your name and deprivation of your private and inalienable rights behind you. Your birth name, your citizenship and <u>inalienable</u> God Given Rights are invaluable and beyond the

understanding, knowledge, comprehension and education of most individuals today.

NOTE: Do not forget, in the U.S. Federal jurisdiction as a fiction _citizen_ you are bound by contracts, statutory legislation and licensing as authorized under *Article 1 Sections 8 and 10 of the U.S. Constitution.* In their federal jurisdiction you are in *Admiralty, Equity* courts and under the Uniform Commercial Code (UCC) and **you are denied your Hawaiian National or American *"common-law"* rights** where your inalienable birth rights *(like freedom of speech, religion, due process, equal protection under the law, the right to, travel, a common-law jury of 12 Peers, etc.)* are preserved. **<u>These rights have been removed along with your birth name!</u>**

The present corporate de facto, Puppet STATE OF HAWAII court systems are lesser U.S. Federalized courts under Article 1 *(of the U.S. Constitution)*. It is obvious that our bankers and elected politicians have modified our court systems and rights for their personal benefit and gain, at the expense of the Hawaiian and American "*Private Citizen's*" inalienable rights to justice.

The choice of citizenship is yours and yours alone. Yes, you still do have choice.

Remember, only *Emancipated Slaves* were given this lesser, government fiction, ***"public citizenship"*** [26] without state's birth rights <u>for a prejudicial reason</u> and were the first wave of United States *"federal citizens"*. We *Hawaiian Nationals,* along with *American Nationals* are presently the second wave. This lesser citizenship is a major deprivation of rights and evidence of very great prejudice and bias by those in power in the Puppet State of Hawaii.

---

26 Public Office. The right, authority, and duty created and conferred by law, by which for a given period, either fixed or by law or enduring the pleasure of the creating power, an individual is invested with some portion of the sovereign functions of government for the benefit of the public. An agency for the state, the duties of which involve in their performance the exercise of some portion of the sovereign power, either great of small. (Black's Law Dict. 6th Ed., Page 1083).

"An unconstitutional act (or actions)
is not law; it confers no rights; it imposes
no duties; affords no protection; it creates
no office; it is in legal contemplation,
as inoperative as though it had
never been passed."

*- Norton vs. Shelby County,
118 US 425 p. 442.*

DUPLICATE U.S. GOVERNMENTS, DUPLICATE U.S. COURTS, AND, DUPLICATE U.S. CITIZENS

THEIR TWO U.S. GOVERNMENTS

The *U.S. Federal Government (military side)* presently holds power over the *de jure* Hawaiian Nation *(remember, there are two United States Governments, the major "National" and the lesser "Federal")*. There are also two American Congresses, *"National"* and *"Federal"*. The President of the United States holds two Offices. One is called the *"Presidency" (National Office; he's presently imitating that Office)* which presides with the National Congress and Government of the Republic. As **"President", he also appoints all the liberal, Godless *(lacking Godly knowledge and Godly values)*, federal judges.** His other lesser Office, <u>but now the primary Office</u>, is that of the senior military commander, functioning as *"Commander-In-Chief"* over the military and its greatly inflated federal jurisdiction. He presently exercises almost all of his authority by using military *(federal)* ***<u>"Executive Orders"</u>***[27]. The

---

27 **Executive order.** (Source: Black's Law Dict. 6th Ed., Page 569) Author's Note: The First Executive Order was issued by Abraham

federal *"Executive Order"* is an order or regulation issued by the President *(almost exclusively - acting as the Commander-In-Chief)* or by some administrative authority under his direction for the purpose of interpreting, implementing, or giving administrative effect to a provision of the Constitution or of some law or treaty. **To have the effect of law, such orders must be published in the *"Federal Register"*[28]**

THEIR TWO AMERICAN SUPREME COURTS

There are also two Supreme Courts, the *"One Supreme Court"* under the *American Constitution of the Republic (An Article III Court - PRESENTLY VACANT)* which is

Lincoln during the Civil War (exigency = urgency; emergency etc.) because he did not have a quorum in Congress with which to pass favorable law. Now used with regularity, regardless of emergency or military need.

28 Federal Register. The Federal Register, published daily, is the medium for making available to the public Federal agency regulations and other legal documents of the executive branch. These documents cover a wide range of Government activities. An important function of the Federal Register is that it includes proposed changes (rules, regulations, standards, etc.) of governmental agencies. Each proposed change published carries an invitation for any citizen or group to participate in the consideration of the proposed regulation through the submission of written data, views, or arguments, and sometimes oral presentations. Such regulations and rules as finally approved appear thereafter in the Code of Federal Regulations. (Source: Black's Law Dict. 6th Ed., Page 612.)

the lawful, competent, rightful and proper Supreme Court for the *American Nation*. Within this very same Constitution there also exists the lesser Article I Section 8 federal jurisdiction court, titled the **United States Supreme Court (Federal)**, which presently is impersonating the greater Constitutional *"One Supreme Court"* of the American Republic and its Union of States.

Additionally, the present federal jurisdiction Article 1 Courts, and lesser courts, agencies etc. will, without your permission and while exceeding their lawful authority, convert your proper birth name on legal documents to the ALL CAPITALIZED printed fiction name. This is done in order bring you under their federal jurisdiction of legislated laws as a *"public citizen"* of Washington D.C. Note: The rightful, *Positive law, American 48 Star Flag of the Republic* does not fly in their Godless courtrooms.

THERE ARE
TWO TYPES OF CITIZENS

THE AMERICAN SOVEREIGN

As repeatedly mentioned there are also two

types of citizens: The natural born living soul *(e.g. American National Private Citizen, a sovereign)* a "freeman" under Almighty God with State's birthrights and birth name *(seal)* intact.

THE IMPERSONATOR CITIZEN

There is also the Federal Government <u>created impersonator</u> of that living soul *(a legal fiction),* titled the *"public citizen",* who *(like the Hawaiian National)* <u>by contract,</u> has become burdened and bound with debt *(income taxes).* There is most definitely a spiritual realm. In it there is both good and evil. Isn't the devil a deceiver and impersonator(?)… coming as an angel of light? He is also a lesser being who delights to burden us with error like those who lie, deceive and cheat us.

One confirmation of *<u>abuse of police power</u>* by the federal *(military jurisdiction)* being in control is the simple fact that Hawaiian and American *Private Citizens* <u>in their lawful birth names are dishonored by the U.S. Federal Government and cannot even vote unless they subjugate their birth name and inalienable birth rights. They are</u>

"disfranchised" [29] at the polls!

I was raised to believe that only criminals *(felons)* were denied the right to vote, not those of us who possessed their birth nation citizenship and birth rights. As mentioned, I was also taught the devil was a liar and deceiver... when our politicians and justices do the same work as the devil; it should make you wonder who they work for?

INALIENABLE RIGHTS ARE OF GOD!

Ku'oko'a, ke hanau maoli kulea'a!

"WITHOUT THE EXPRESSION OF RIGHTS, YOU HAVE NO RIGHTS."

- Author

---

29 Disfranchise. To deprive of the rights and privileges of a free citizen; to deprive of chartered rights and immunities; to deprive of any franchise, as of the right of voting in elections, etc... (Source: Black's Law Dict. 6th Ed. Page 468.

Freedom is not free! That
right is secured at a price.

What price are you willing to pay?

"The people are the masters
of both Congress and courts, not to
overthrow the Constitution, but to
overthrow the men who pervert it!"

- Abraham Lincoln

KNOW YOUR HISTORY
AND YOUR RIGHTS

Learn about your government and learn how to lawfully protect yourself and your rights! Your inalienable Hawaiian *"Private Citizen"* birth rights, freedoms and liberties are at stake! This is your responsibility in order that you and your children can be protected from greater government abuse, bondage and tyrannical actions by unethical people using deceptive government civil service practices. Learn the truth about your citizenship and birthrights and then properly and lawfully reclaim them and execute them if you are functioning as a foreign U.S. Federal *"citizen"* under a *"legal fiction"* name.

If you check your birth name on your de facto Driver's License, U.S. Social Security Card, Credit Cards, and Birth Certificate and find that your birth name has been changed, you are foreign to your *Hawaiian National Government* and its Constitution; and/or the *American Constitution of the Republic.* If you are American born you are also foreign to your sovereign State's birth rights *(common-law of your birth State).*

You would therefore not have *"inalienable"* birth rights. Surprised? You should be.

**DO YOU REALLY KNOW
WHAT COUNTRY
YOU WERE BORN IN?**

OUR EDUCATORS, OUR JURISTS AND OUR CIVIL SERVANTS:

Today, liberal educators in our Puppet Hawaii State public school systems profit most from devious federal and state assistance grants *(hush-money or "buy-off" money)*. Their students seeking knowledge and denied truth, do not profit. These educators, et al, teach and do what the feds tell them to teach and do, and they will not bite the hand that feeds them *(with our taxes)*. I fault our liberal, weak minded educators for the *"Dumbing"* down of our children of Hawaii and America. I also find that our judicial systems consisting of inept administrators, attorneys, and judges, being Godless, are far removed from the reality of our Hawaiian and American Constitutions and People they are bound *(under oaths of Office)* to serve. All these, as groupings appear to have sold their souls, compromised their values and the values of our great country for temporal gain of personal prestige, position, prestige of community, or money. They've either abandoned, compromised, or maybe even sold their integrity, *(assuming that they had some in the first place)* and the positive evidences are the corrupted values of many generations of our young children... all because they refuse to teach and honor God and His Truth. They refuse to look at us, the People as the source of their personal gain. Instead, they're repeatedly chummed with enticements *(our tax dollars)* and look to the corrupt, irresponsible, bankrupt U.S. Federal Government for handouts ($$$$$) to pay and maintain themselves in their carnal, but limited lifestyles, allowing themselves to be in constant federal bondage to corruption, misguided philosophies, estranged truths and outright deceptions. This same type of thinking has permeated our politicians and civil servants to where they think that because they can irresponsibly manipulate with money they can now rule and control us with debt *(federal note)* paper dollars instead of us ruling and controlling them. Our elected politicians and judges, government officials, and civil servants from Washington D.C. to the lowest level of our local communities are primarily self-serving, and have become fearless and arrogant. They function in deceitfulness.

TESTING OF BIRTH NAME
AND BIRTH RIGHTS IN
COURTS OF LAW

The properly spelled birth right name versus the printed ALL CAPITALIZED legal fiction name has been affirmed as to the distinguishing of jurisdiction, at law, in the following *United States Court for the Hawaii District*[30] cases:

> 96-01177; 97-00239; 97-01050; 98-00089; 98-00252; 98-00418; 98-00574; 00-00048; Also, Los Angeles Superior Court – Central District, Case No. BS-052162 (Sept. 2, 1998)

It has also been tested in dozens of de facto *(unlawful, but in power)* Puppet STATE OF HAWAII District Court cases. These herein stated facts of truth have never been refuted nor proven wrong in any of the filed and documented cases of record. The fact is that judges within both the *de facto* Puppet

---

30 U.S. Court for the Hawaii District. The supposedly lawful court's jurisdiction does not include the Islands of the Hawaiian Archipelago (affirmed by U.S. law in Title 28 USC Section 91) and its judges are under modified, fraudulent oaths of Office that are not in compliance with Title 28 USC 453.

STATE OF HAWAII courts and the *U.S. Federal Court for the Hawaii District*, exercise full collusive participation with Attorneys *(Members of the Bar Association)* and *U.S. Justice Department* attorneys in <u>open violation of law</u>, in order to capture jurisdiction over the *"Hawaiian National"* and *"American National"* living souls *(the natural man)* by unlawfully converting the properly spelled, English language birth name to the improper *"legal fiction"* name in their court filings. This outrageous ignoring, abuse and denial of rights to justice, private rights, and dishonoring the truth of law, is done as if these legalists are under a great devious and demonic secret oath, greater than that lawfully required under U.S. law, specifically, **28 U.S.C. § 453** to honor Almighty God and Country.

We assume all justices and attorneys have supposedly taken oath to honor Almighty God and Country for the American People; as required under their Constitution, Treaties *(Supreme law)*; and laws *(to protect all types of citizens)*. **Yet, they have not and do not!**

In the de facto, Puppet STATE OF HAWAII, there is no judicial oath or commitment to honor Almighty God. Therefore, attorneys sworn in by these *"bastard oath"* judges are also of questionable commitment to righteousness.

Justice has been prostituted! A questionable, Godless, judicial system, <u>including attorneys,</u> has permitted the concealment and theft of our birth rights! They have diminished and squelched our freedoms and liberties! Today, these judges and attorneys believe their law is their god and that they are greater than Almighty God! They do not know our God or His ways and most definitely do not call on Him or seek His Word for guidance. They are fools because they do not respect Him and by their actions say, *"There is no God!"*

The Lord God says in *Isaiah, Chapter 59,* *"...justice is turned away backward, and righteousness stands afar off; for truth has fallen in to the street (gutter) and equity cannot enter."*

<u>The American judicial system has become a lesser, foreign "federalized" political injustice system</u>. It no longer is a true, just justice system that honors the sovereign States of the Union, American Constitution or its *National Citizens.* The massive political

corruption of America's judicial system and its influence over Hawaiians is caused by Americans failure as individuals and as a free People to seek awareness, knowledge, understanding, and respect for protection of their own rights. They have also failed in supervision of their national, State and local justice systems. They have refused to stand up and fight for their freedoms; and righteousness; to protect their children and their children's children.

We are all failures! We have not stood up for the *"righteousness"* [31] *of Almighty God*!

---

31 Righteous. 1. characterized by uprightness or morality: a righteous observance of the law. 2. morally right or justifiable: righteous indignation. 3. acting in an upright, moral way; virtuous: a righteous and godly person.... (Source: Webster's Encyclopedic Unabridged Dictionary, 2001 Ed.) Author's Note: The words "righteous" and "righteousness" DO NOT APPEAR in Black's Law Dictionary. That should tell us something about our legal system.

CHANGING OF BABIES BIRTH NAMES ON BIRTH CERTIFICATES

The U.S. Federalized corporate jurisdictions *(E.g. the de facto Puppet Hawaiian State Government which includes its county, municipal and state agencies)* unlawfully and deliberately convert birth names of babies and minors into the printed ALL CAPITAL-IZED *"legal fiction"* name <u>without the explicit consent</u>, knowledge and awareness of the parents for a reason. This action under law, previously mentioned, is called *"constructive fraud"* because it's premeditated to gain a legal citizenship advantage over the child. The parents of this post-war generation of children *(since World War II)* have been kept ignorant *(e.g. not taught the truth by our liberal tax paid educators in grammar schools, high schools and colleges about their fundamental and inalienable rights and the power and freedoms possessed in their lawful birth names).* These precious children, ill taught and lacking knowledge, are later in life easily misled by others to be bound by contracts that take away and keep away their freedoms and inalienable rights.

UNLAWFUL NAME CHANGERS

These ignorant politicians and civil servants, without fear of retribution, deliberately change the names of babies on birth certificates when registering them in the Department of Health *(Commerce)* of the de facto Puppet State. They make the living soul *(baby)* a property or *"thing"* of the subordinate federal jurisdiction. When the parents who have the legal and lawful right to stop the procedure do not, but condone it by ignorance, they have in fact given *(permitted legal adoption, acquiesced, submitted)* their babies to the State. Yet, the parents still have the responsibility to raise that child within the de facto State *(as the State dictates)*, at the expense of the righteousness and inalienable rights granted us by Almighty God.

In the *de facto* Puppet STATE, the lawful and proper English language spelled names of babies are <u>unlawfully changed</u> to fictions by de facto corporate agencies *(hospitals, health care agencies, etc.)* and their de facto Department of Health actively participates in ongoing fraud against the Hawaiian People, and others.

SILENT, ACTIVE IDENTITY THEFT

The names are changed to ALL CAPITALIZED *"legal fictions"* in violation of law and right <u>without the parent's explicit understanding</u> and knowledge as to the consequences of such change. <u>This is outright identity theft, corruption and fraud by the de facto State</u>! This fact is easily confirmed. The only reason for doing so is to make the innocent child a *"ward of the State" (legally, but not lawfully adopted)* ignoring lawful birthrights and authority of the parents.

In Hawaii, it removes the child from under the de jure *"Hawaiian Kingdom National Constitution",* their natural birth rights and National *"common-law"...* and makes them foreign, second-class 14th Amendment United States *"public citizens" (things, without birth rights)* of the U.S. Federal jurisdiction while they are still domiciled on their own Hawaiian National birth soil. This fraud is deviously exercised through our ignorance, to take away rights whether we are Hawaiian or American! In America, it removes the child from under most of the *American Constitution* placing them under

Article 1, Section 8 (federal jurisdiction) of that same Constitution, as *"public c̲itizens"* of Washington, D.C.

CONTRACTS THAT CHANGE LIVES

Contracts entered into, <u>with knowledge</u>, are binding upon those who enter into them. In the *de facto* STATE OF HAWAII and Federal United States, I believe that the citizenship change, or <u>contract</u>, is accomplished by entering into and accepting foreign state adhesions *(e.g. driver's licenses, identification cards, etc.);* and with federal contracts... primarily the implied *federal <u>"adhesion contract"</u>*[32] *(called the **Social Security Act** which is affirmed by your signature [seal] and acceptance of a Social Identification Number and Card).*

Today, even our U.S. Passport names are unlawfully modified <u>without our specific</u>

---

32 Adhesion contract. Standardized contract form offered to consumers of goods and services on essentially "take it or leave it" basis without affording consumer realistic opportunity to bargain and under such conditions that consumer cannot obtain desired product or services except by acquiescing in form contract. Distinctive feature of adhesion contract is that weaker party has no realistic choice as to its terms.... Recognizing that these contracts are not the result of traditionally "bargained" contracts, the trend is to relieve parties from onerous conditions imposed by such contracts. However, not every such contract is unconscionable... (Source: Black's Law Dict. 6th Ed., Page 40)

authorization and consent and used to violate our lawful birth rights, falsely revealing to the world that we are bound, enslaved *"citizens"* of the federal jurisdiction and not free born as *"Hawaiian National"* or *"American National" "Private Citizens"*.

CITIZENSHIP IS VOLUNTARY

WHAT DID YOU DO WITH YOUR BIRTH RIGHTS?

WHAT ARE YOU GOING TO DO WITH YOUR BIRTH RIGHTS?

"Good men, without knowledge of their
government that provides them freedom,
shall soon loose their freedom and
liberty only to be enslaved, because of
indifference and ignorance."

- Author

SELLING YOUR CHILD'S
BIRTH CERTIFICATE
FOR FINANCIAL GAIN

THE MORTGAGED CITIZEN

Your <u>corporate, federalized state</u> *(Hawaii is not a sovereign State of the American Union of States, only a federal corporation)* takes your modified name birth certificate, places a monetary border around it, and creates a banker's ***"Bearer Bond"***[33] and ***"Bearer Instrument"***[34] which is also a ***"Bearer Document"***[35] mortgaging you under their fiction name *(which you have endorsed as yours)* to the U.S Federal Treasury *(**Federal Reserve**[36])* as a debtor. My belief is that this

---

33 Bearer Bond. Bonds payable to the person having possession of them. Such bonds do not require endorsement to transfer ownership but only the transfer of possession. (Source: Black's Law Dict. 6th Ed. Page 154)

34 Bearer instrument. An instrument is payable to bearer when by its terms it is payable to (a) bearer or the order of bearer; or (b) a specified person or bearer; or (c) "cash" or the order of "cash", or any other indication which does not purport to designate a specific payee. U.C.C. §§ 3-111, 3-204(2). (Source: Black's Law Dict. 6th Ed. Page 154)

35 Bearer document. A document that runs to bearer upon issuance or after a blank endorsement, and that is negotiated by delivery alone. U.C.C. §§ 7-501(1) & (2)(a), Anyone in possession of a bearer document is a holder of it. U.C.C § 1-201(20) (Source: Black's Law Dict. 6th Ed., Page 154)

36 Federal Reserve. (Author's Note) The Federal Reserve is a private pure trust of bankers, et al, given authority and power to run and control the American monetary system under the U.S. Treasury by

77

maneuver also transfers your now modified birth certificate to Washington, D.C. *(U.S. Treasury)* so as to convert you into a debtor *"citizen"* of Washington, D.C., <u>at least on paper</u>. You are now a <u>mortgaged</u>, U.S. Federal *"public citizen", person"* or *"thing"* outside of the *Hawaiian Constitution* and *American Constitution of the Republic*, <u>without birth rights</u>. This conversion under law, as previously mentioned, is called *"constructive fraud"* of the highest order, because bankers and politicians in present power do it with fullness of knowledge and with the intent to deceive; a premeditated scheme of the highest corrupt, criminal sort.

HOW IT WORKS

Here's the deal. As I see it, if on a document you use their fictitious name that they own, and upon which you ignorantly placed your guarantee *(your "Seal" = "Signature")* to honor that document, you have contracted. Now, the U.S. Federal Treasury *(e.g. Federal Reserve)* can assess / place a debt upon their fiction name that you are using, let's say, $500,000.00 to more than $1,000,000.00.

---

then President Franklin D. Roosevelt through the Federal Reserve Act of 1933.

Now you in your lifetime must pay the *"federal money god" (e.g. bankers)* by way of the Internal Revenue Service (IRS) the assessed income taxes *(lien)* <u>for the privilege</u> of using their name. You have now, with your signatured consent, transferred yourself into their federal jurisdiction by acceptance and use of their name... getting the picture? Assuming that your birth certificate is also modified and pledged by your state as security, you have become willingly a paper Federal U.S. *"public citizen"* of Washington D.C., a federal enclave.

Ke Akua Mana Loa a'ole maka'u!

CITIZENSHIP IS VOLUNTARY

U.S. FEDERAL INCOME TAXES:

APPLY TO THE <u>CREATED</u> 14TH AMENDMENT, U.S. FEDERAL"<u>c</u>itizens" ("EMANCIPATED SLAVES") AND ALL OTHER U.S. GOVERNMENT <u>CREATED</u> FICTION ENTITIES; RESIDING WITHIN THE <u>LIMITED</u>, U.S. FEDERAL JURISDICTION.

<u>FOREIGN INCOME TAXES DO NOT APPLY TO HAWAIIAN NATIONALS</u> UNDER THEIR NATIONAL COMMON-LAW AND NATURAL BIRTHRIGHTS; WHILE DOMICILED ON THEIR OWN SOVEREIGN AINA.

CONCLUSION:

ABOUT IRS "INCOME TAXES" AND THE FICTION CITIZEN

The proof of the pudding is in the eating!

If you, a *"Hawaiian National"*, and *"Private Citizen"*, <u>are not</u> under the printed ALL CAPITALIZED *"legal fiction"* name *(having reclaimed your inalienable birth rights)* and their foreign fifty star *federal military* flag *(stepped out from under their flag jurisdiction)* you do not owe and are not liable for U.S. Federal Income Taxes, any more than any other foreign *Private Citizen* living on his own national birth soil. That is, unless you *"elected" (contracted)* to.

Foreign nationals do not owe U.S. income tax if they do not earn their living directly from the U.S. Federal Government sources *(Government payrolls, contracts, ect.)*. If you earn income from those sources, you are obligated by contract, and owe them the contracted tax amount; otherwise as a *"Private Citizen"* you are a *"free man"* and only owe taxes to your lawful Hawaiian National Government, not some foreign, unlawful occupying government on your Hawaiian owned land. If you are a lesser U.S. *"citizen"* or U.S. Federal *"Taxpayer"*, by contract you are obligated to pay U.S. income taxes.

Regarding ***"Income Tax"***[37]; please read closely, ***Footnote #37***. Under U.S. law, you will find that there is no *"income tax"* on *"Private Citizens"*, e.g. *"Nationals"*. *"Income Tax"* therefore only applies to created, fiction *federal corporate officers* or *"public citizens"*, e.g. *"slaves"* who hold the government Office of ***"Taxpayer"***[38] in their federal jurisdiction.

"Hawaiian National Private Citizens", are foreigners to the U.S. Federal government jurisdiction while domiciled on their own national birth soil and are lawfully not

37 **Income tax.** A tax on the yearly profits arising from property, professions, trades and offices. 2 Steph. Comm. 573 (Source: Black's Law Dict. 1st Ed. Page 611) "Income tax." A tax on the yearly profit arising from property, professions, trades, and offices. 2 Steph. Comm. 573. Levi v. Louisville, 97 Ky. 394, 30 S. W. 973, 28 L. R. A. 480; Parker v. Insurance Co., 42 La. Ann. 428 7 South. 599. (Source: Black's Law Dict. 2nd Ed. Page 612) NOT FOUND IN THE 6TH EDITION OF BLACK'S LAW DICTIONARY. DO YOU WONDER WHY?

38 **Taxpayer.** A person whose income is subject to taxation; one from whom government demands a pecuniary contribution towards its support. (Black's Law Dict. 6th Ed., Page 1459) (Author's Note: "Person" in this sense would be a federal, created entity, or "citizen".)

taxable. U.S. law doesn't apply to Hawaiian Nationals *(who are foreigners to the U.S. jurisdiction and are domiciled on foreign soil)*.

As mentioned previously, the Hawaiian *"national"* citizenship never changed under the Organic Act *(Territory of Hawaii Act of 1900)* or the Statehood Act *(of 1959)*! Hawaiians have always been and still are nationals… <u>unless</u> you have given, yielded *(contracted)* away your birth name rights. **Unfortunately, the *Hawaiian <u>federal</u> "<u>citizen</u>"* who lives in the Islands** (one who has given his birth rights away) **is just another bound U.S. *"Taxpayer" (federal office held)* in the U.S. Federal military flag jurisdiction, without any rights. They <u>must pay</u> their <u>contracted</u> tax liability!**

THE FOLLOWING APPLIES TO AMERICAN NATIONALS

THE FOLLOWING IS FOR YOUR AWARENESS AND KNOWLEDGE

<u>American National Private Citizens are obligated to honor Positive law. The *Internal Revenue Code (IRS)* is not "Positive law"</u> as per IRS admission in **Title 26 of the United**

States Code, Section 7806 (a) and (b).

Please read: <u>I now quote Section 7806</u>:

"Construction of Title (Title 26, IRS Code) (a) The cross references in this title to other portions of the title, or other provisions of law, where the word "see" is used, are made only for convenience, and shall be given no legal effect. (b) No inference, implication, or presumption of legislative construction shall be drawn or made by reason of the location or grouping of any particular section or provision or portion of this title, nor shall any table of contents, table of cross references, or similar outline, analysis, or descriptive matter relating to the contents of this title be given any legal effect. The preceding sentence also applies to the side notes and ancillary tables contained in the various prints of this Act before its enactment into law." (Source '96 Title 26 USC Code)

I repeat, the IRS Code has never been "... *enacted into Positive law"* **(e.g. read into the** *"Federal Register"* **so as to become** *Positive law).*

American National Private Citizens (sovereigns) are bound by righteousness under Almighty God and obligated to honor *Positive law*, not the banker's demonic federal statutory impersonation of law. The *Internal Revenue Code (IRS)* is therefore only suggestion to *American Nationals*! The IRS Code only applies to U.S. Federal created *"public citizens"* or *"persons"* within *their lesser, subordinate jurisdiction.* **So IF you are a *"National"*, a *"State's born sovereign"*, functioning under your properly spelled, lawful birth name, why do you want to honor corruption?** Are you intimidated? Are you fearful?

Fear is not from Almighty God!

Americans, have you forgotten? The 16th Amendment to the U.S. Constitution *(for a national income tax)* was never ratified by the sovereign American States! It only applies to the U.S. jurisdiction of Washington D.C. and their *"citizens"*.

THE FOLLOWING IS
FOR HAWAIIAN NATIONALS

My deduction, based upon actions of the Internal Revenue Service (IRS) and other agencies including the *U.S. Federal Courts* is that the printed ALL CAPITALIZED name denotes a *"person"* endued with *"Public Office"* in their federal jurisdiction as a ***"Public Official"***[39] *e.g.* ***"Taxpayer"***[40]. That being the case, it is my conclusion that this would be sufficient IRS justification for their lack of / or need for, proper, lawful service; and, further justify their abusive use of unsigned liens, <u>assuming that the Public Office held by you is that of a U.S. Federal Government *"Taxpayer"*</u>.

BEWARE THE DECEIVERS

Do you still want to continue to be a foreign, second-class, U.S. Federal *"citizen"* on your own national aina?

Don't forget, you still have lawful choice!

---

39 Public Official. An officer; a person invested with the authority of an office. (Source: Black's Law Dict. 6th Ed. Page 1084.) Author's Note: The official, designated government office of "Taxpayer" would be appropriate for this justification. SEE "Person", Footnote 24.

40 Taxpayer. A person whose income is subject to taxation; one from whom government demands a pecuniary contribution towards its support. (Black's Law Dict. 6th Ed., Page 1459) (Author's Note: "Person" in this sense would be a federal, created entity, or "citizen".)

ENOUGH ABOUT THE IRS
AND INCOME TAXES

Remember, there is much to learn about your birth name and birth rights which affirm your freedoms. Get knowledge and get wisdom. It all starts with how you spell your name *(your lawful seal and identity)* and, what you accept by contract and become obligated for.

Remember: The *"Private Citizen"* is <u>a *free man*</u> under God and the other is still a ***"bond servant"***[41] *(Emancipated Slave)* who is now under federal license. If you are using their printed ALL CAPITALIZED name out of ignorance and want to restore your birth rights, <u>you must do it properly</u>. There is a lawfully proper way to do all things. **Remember, your inalienable birth rights are preserved and retained in your properly spelled birth name! Now that.... is truth!**

Godless money seeking attorneys and corrupt judges within the Puppet Hawaii federal legal system will tell us: ***"Ignorance***

---

[41] **Bond servant.** 1. a person who serves in bondage; slave. 2. a person bound to service without wages. (Source: Webster's Encyclopedic Dict. 2001 Ed.) Author's Note: Not found in Black's Law Dictionary.

of the law is no excuse!" These are the very same who hide that knowledge of truth and law from us.

It is time for Hawaiians to seek greater knowledge and wisdom in order to not be deceived. **Knowledge is power!** Wisdom is how to use that power.

Hawaiians still have choice and can live anywhere in this world they want. To do so, they must honor those particular countries laws and their people's rights, customs and traditions!

In Hawaii, it is time for ho'oponopono of the various Hawaiian groups; and, for a major, positive, constructive, political change in Hawaii Nei.

**Iesu Cristo ke ala,
ke olaio a ke ola hou.**

Dated: March 21, 2009

Respectfully,

Aran Alton: Ardaiz,
American National and
Private Citizen

FOR ADDITIONAL INFORMATION:

Contact:
The Truth of God Ministry
Email: *TruthofGodMinistry@Hawaii.rr.com*

Other books by Aran Alton Ardaiz:

HAWAII: The Fake State

AMERICAN BIRTHRIGHTS:
Understanding "American National"
Private Citizen Birth Rights

"Woe to those judges who issue
unrighteous decrees, and to the magistrates
who keep causing unjust and oppressive
decisions to be recorded, to turn aside the
needy from justice and to make plunder
of the rightful claim of the poor of My
people, that widows may be their spoil,
and that they may make
the fatherless their prey!

(Holy Bible, Isaiah 10: 1, 2

Printed in the United States
149442LV00002B/1/P